BLOOM™

A Collection of Fabric Flowers

Edited by Sharon Frank

Annie's™

Table of Contents

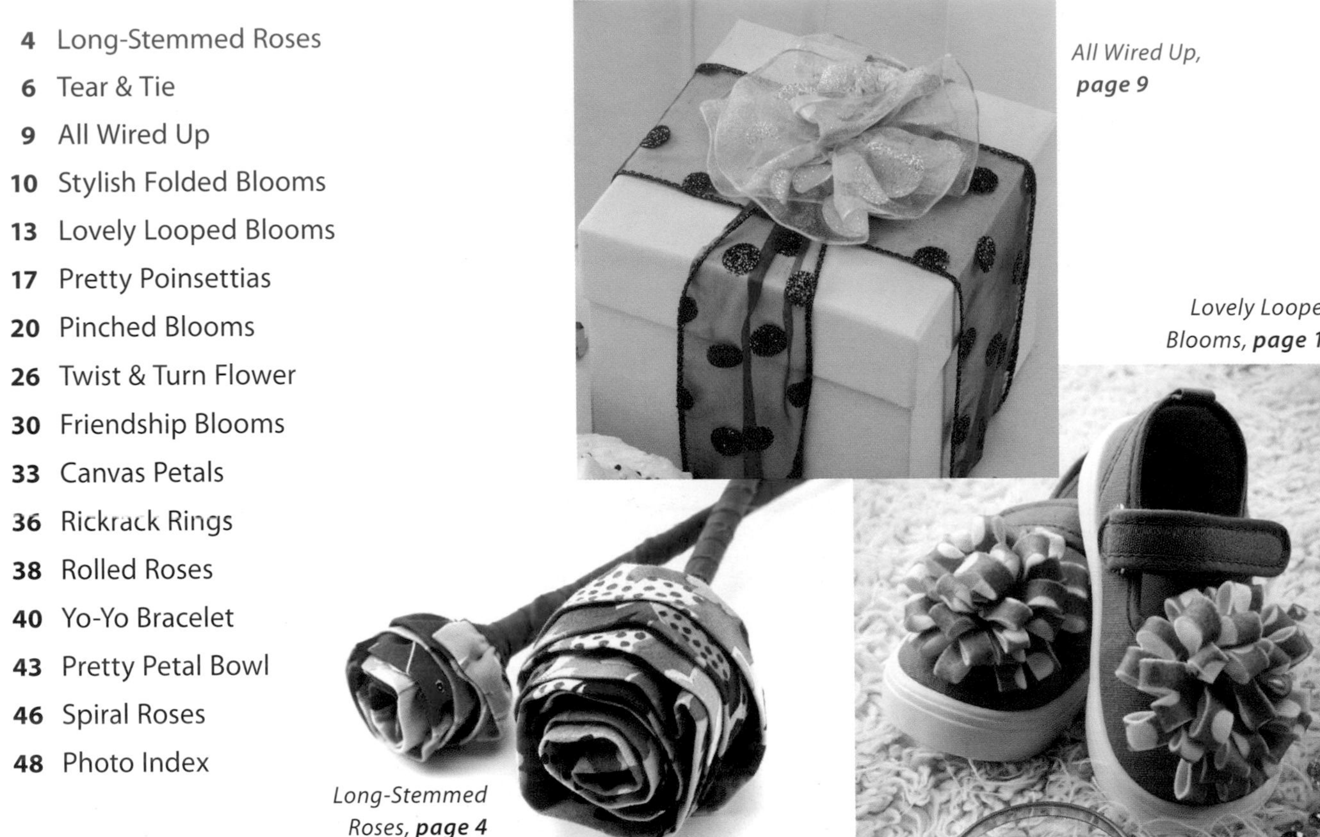

All Wired Up, ***page 9***

Lovely Looped Blooms, ***page 13***

Long-Stemmed Roses, ***page 4***

Tips

Fabric suggestions *have been made for each flower, but within those suggestions are plenty of possibilities. Be adventurous; try making some of the flowers from scraps in your fabric stash.*

Borrow a trick from quilters: *Use freezer paper as a template material when you see it listed. When making templates for shapes, trace the pattern shapes onto the dull side of freezer paper and cut out. The shiny side of the freezer paper will stick to fabric when ironed. These can be reused up to six times.*

Use good-quality polyester thread, *and for the most part, medium-length hand-sewing needles. Thread is not listed in the materials lists. We assume you will have coordinating colors on hand to use.*

Treating some fabrics *with a liquid fabric stiffener makes them easier to cut and bend. For cotton, brush the liquid stiffener onto both sides of fabric with foam brush, following the manufacturer's directions. Allow to dry completely. Wool and felt do not need to be treated.*

Bloom—A Collection of Fabric Flowers

Bloom is all about creating beautiful fabric flowers to help your projects blossom into something even more fabulous! In this book, we will guide you through 15 fun and easy projects to create fabric and ribbon flowers that will maximize your opportunities to embellish and enliven.

We love fabric flowers, and obviously many other people do too! What is it about them that makes us smile? Just as a real flower opens up and inspires when it blossoms, fabric flowers can open up and inspire you and those around you.

Give a friend or loved one a beautiful fabric flower as a way of saying, "I'm thinking of you." Brighten up any outfit, handbag or headband by adding a flower. In this book you'll find them used for jewelry, on flip-flops, for home decor and more! The creative possibilities are endless!

Fabric and ribbon are just waiting to be cut, sewn, folded, dipped or ruffled. Whether it's a bold floral print or a subtle soft pink, fabric can inspire—and it usually does!

Our question and challenge to you is, how will YOU be inspired to use these flowers? We can't wait to see what you will do!

All our best,

Kim & Kris

Kim and Kris are identical twin sisters, and in 2010, they began hosting the popular online show *The DIY Dish*. Their weekly show features craft- and fabric-related projects for home decor, accessories, quilts, embroidery and more.

Kim Christopherson is the founder of www.YouCanMakeThis.com, www.SWAKembroidery.com and www.theDIYdish.com. When starting the sites, Kim wanted to provide a place where people could learn how to make items for their homes and families. She has always loved the creative process and the joy it brings, and she loves to see others do the same.

Kim is also the owner and creative force of Kimberbell Designs, a popular sewing, quilt and embroidery design pattern company. Kimberbell products are available online and in quilt and fabric shops around the country.

Kris Thurgood owns My Girlfriend's Quilt Shoppe and My Girlfriend's Attic retreat center located in Logan, Utah.

Kim and Kris have also been featured on national television shows including *The Rachael Ray Show* and *The Nate Berkus Show*. You'll find them in magazines, such as *Where Women Create, Designs in Machine Embroidery,* and they write a regular column in *Where Women Cook* magazine. They are also monthly contributors to the local NBC affiliate lifestyle television show *Studio 5*. In 2011, they were named among the top 40 (No. 6 and No. 7!) women entrepreneurs by LaunchHER.

Long-Stemmed Roses

Finished Size
Varies

Materials
- Scraps dark green
- ⅛ yard woven fabric dark green solid (optional)
- ¼ yard woven fabric for flower
- ⅛–¼-inch-diameter 12–18-inch-long fallen tree sticks or dowel rod
- Basic sewing supplies and equipment

Tips

A quarter of a yard of fabric will make one large rose and two smaller roses. Three quarters of a yard of fabric will make four large and eight small roses.

For a multicolored bouquet, cut strips separately from coordinating fabric scraps. You will need 4 x 42-inch strips for large roses and 2 x 22-inch strips for small roses.

Cutting

From flower fabric:
- Cut one 4-inch by fabric width strip for large rose.
- Cut one 2-inch by fabric width strip; subcut strip into two 2 x 22-inch strips for small roses.

From dark green scraps:
- Cut three 1 x 4-inch strips.

From dark green solid (optional):
- Cut four 1-inch by fabric width strips.

Assembly
1. Fold and press both short ends of large rose strip to wrong side and then press in half lengthwise, wrong sides together.

2. Hand-sew a line of gathering stitches ½ inch apart and ¼ inch from raw edges of folded strip (Figure 1). Backstitch at beginning and leave long thread tail at end.

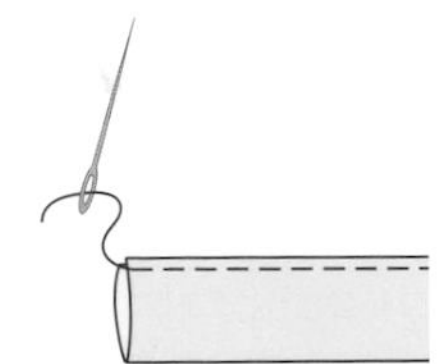

Figure 1

Tip

Hand-sewn gathering stitches will make a very loose rose. If you want tighter roses to mix with these, machine-sew the gathering stitches with long basting stitches.

3. Gently pull thread tail to loosely gather strip up to approximately one half its original length.

4. Hot-glue one end of strip to the top of the small stick or dowel rod with long folded edge just above top of stick or rod (Figure 2).

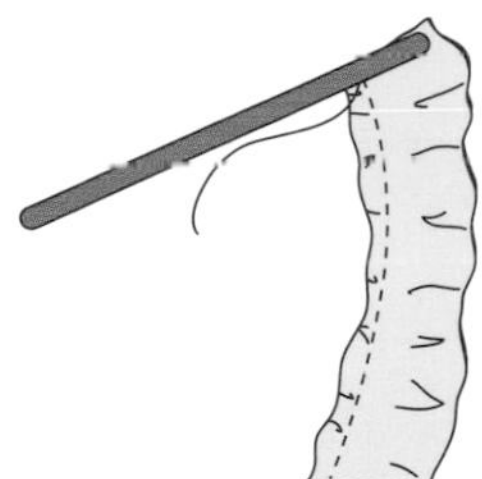

Figure 2

5. Wrap gathered fabric strip around end of stick or dowel rod, tacking in place with hot-glue every ½–1 inch (Figure 3).

Figure 3

6. Wrap and hot-glue 1 x 4-inch strip dark green around bottom of rose to cover raw edges.

7. If using dowel rod for stem, wrap and hot-glue 1-inch by fabric width strip dark green solid to the bottom of rose to cover raw edges and continue wrapping strip to cover dowel rod, pulling snugly and hot-gluing at end to secure.

8. Repeat all steps with 2-inch-wide woven fabric strips for small roses. ■

Tear & Tie

Finished Size
Approximately 4 inches in diameter

Materials
- Scraps craft felt
- ⅛ yard woven fabric
- Plastic rings: ¾-inch and 1-inch
- 1 (1-inch) decorative button
- Hot-glue gun and glue sticks
- Basic sewing supplies and equipment

Cutting
From woven fabric:
- Cut or tear four ¾-inch by fabric width strips. Cut strips into 25 (¾ x 5-inch) strips.

From scraps craft felt:
- Cut one 1¼-inch-diameter circle using pattern provided.

Tips
Because you want the fabric to fray in this project, choose light- to medium-weight woven fabric like 100-percent cotton, satin or silk.

Raid your scraps to cut the small pieces needed.

Assembly
1. Divide fabric strips into one group of 10 strips and one group of 15 strips.

2. Select the ¾-inch plastic ring and group of 10 fabric strips.

3. Tie center of each fabric strip to the plastic ring with a simple knot (Figure 1). Adjust tied strips around the ring evenly to look like petals.

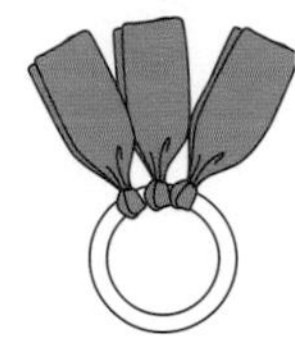

Figure 1

4. Trim petals to approximately 1 inch from plastic ring (Figure 2). Set aside.

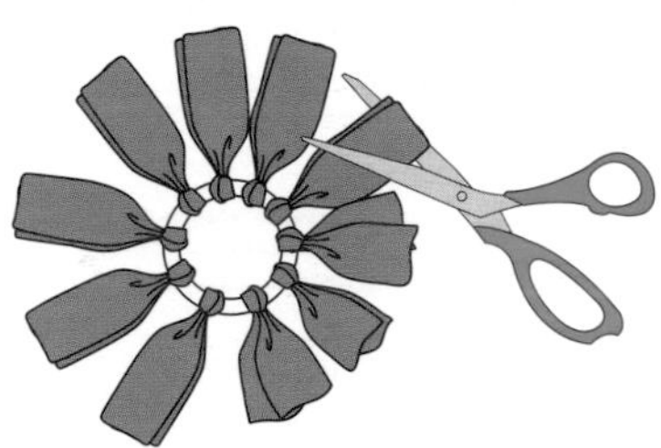

Figure 2

5. Repeat step 3 with 1-inch plastic ring and group of 15 fabric strips to make a second flower layer (Figure 3). Do not trim petals.

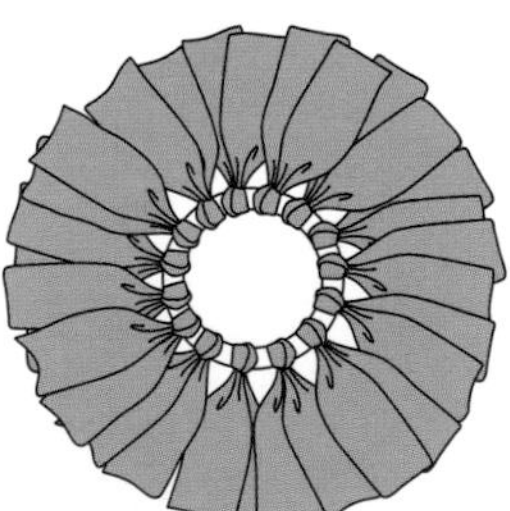

Figure 3

6. Hot-glue the ¾-inch-ring flower layer to the center of the 1-inch-ring flower layer. Trim petals of 1-inch-ring flower layer as desired.

7. Hot-glue the felt circle to the center of the 1-inch-ring side of the flower.

8. Hot-glue decorative button to flower center on ¾-inch ring side.

Tear & Tie Necklace

You Will Need

- 36-inch or longer purchased heavy necklace or necklace chain
- 2 Tear & Tie Blooms
- Tape
- Hot-glue gun and glue sticks

Assembly

1. Make two Tear & Tie Blooms. Trim the 1-inch layer even with the ¾-inch layer on one bloom and leave the 1-inch layer untrimmed on the other.

2. While wearing necklace or chain, mark where blooms are to be attached with tape.

3. Hot-glue flowers to necklace at tape, positioning flowers to touch or overlap. ■

Tip

Because of their weight, position the blooms in the upper chest area, like on the project shown, or position three to five blooms at the bottom loop of necklace.

Tear & Tie
Circle Template
Cut as per instructions

All Wired Up

Finished Size
Approximately 4 inches in diameter

Materials
- 1 yard 1-inch-wide wire-edge ribbon
- Basic sewing supplies and equipment

Assembly
1. Fold one end of ribbon in half lengthwise with wired edges of ribbon at top.

2. Gather-stitch 9 inches at center of folded ribbon end, taking a few backstitches at beginning to secure (Figure 1).

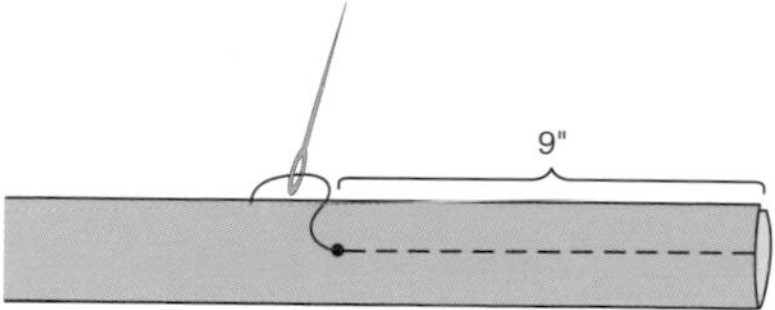

Figure 1

3. Gently pull the thread to gather the ribbon end into a ball as shown in Figure 2.

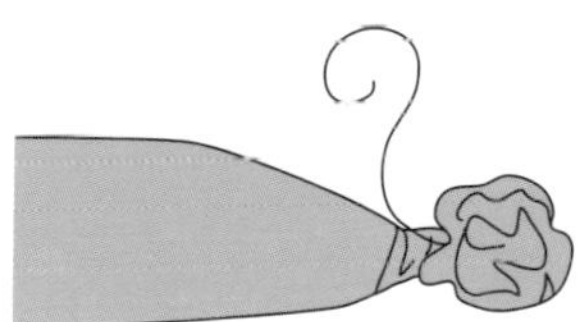

Figure 2

4. Shape gathered section into a ball and take a few stitches through the ball with the gathering thread to secure. Knot and trim thread tail.

5. With ribbon ball to one side and remaining ribbon length flat, gently pull only the bottom-edge wire to gather (Figure 3).

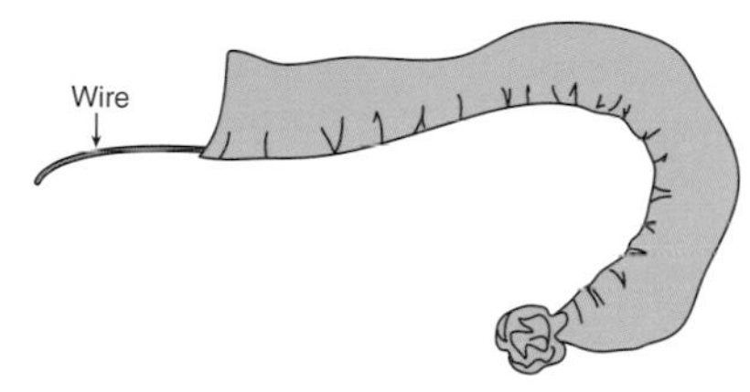

Figure 3

6. Gather and wrap the ribbon length around the ribbon ball to create flower petals.

7. Adjust length around the ribbon ball to create a flower referring to project photo. Stitch the ribbon length in place close to the bottom wired edge. Trim excess wire from ribbon end. ■

Tip

To make larger or smaller flowers, use wider or narrower wire-edge ribbon. Crimp the un-gathered wired ribbon edge to shape your flowers even more.

Stylish Folded Blooms

Finished Size
3½ inches in diameter

Materials
***Note:** Materials listed make two 3½-inch blooms.*
- 18 x 22-inch piece (or ¼ yard) fabric
- Hot-glue gun and glue sticks (optional)
- 1–1½-inch-wide decorative button (optional)
- Basic sewing supplies and equipment

Assembly
1. Using pattern provided, trace and cut 10 circles from fabric. ***Note:** These flowers can be made from any woven fabric, or craft or wool felt. Choose your fabric considering the item the flowers will be attached to, its use and whether you want the item to be dressed up or down.*

2. Fold one circle in half, wrong sides together (Figure 1).

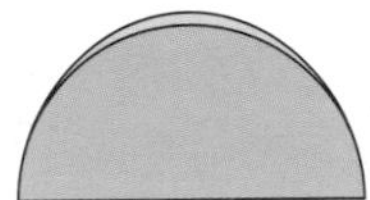

Figure 1

3. Referring to Figure 2, fold half circle in half again to make a petal.

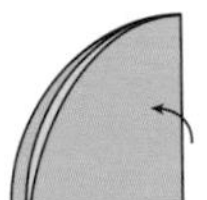

Figure 2

4. Position petal on right side of flat base circle with folded point toward circle center (Figure 3). If stitching together, take a few small stitches through the point of the folded petal into the base. If using glue, place a small dot of hot-glue at the point of the petal base and a small drop inside the fold near the point to secure the petal from unfolding.

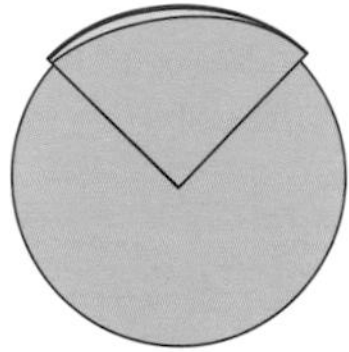

Figure 3

5. Continue to make and add a total of four petals to the base circle following steps 2–4.

6. Add another round of four petals, stitching or hot-gluing between the petals of the first layer to fill the base circle, referring to flower photos on page 12.

7. Fold the last circle in half and roll into a cone. Stitch or hot-glue cone in flower center or stitch a decorative button at flower center to complete. ■

Tip

Change the size of the circles to make blooms that "fit" with the item you are decorating. Make larger blooms by using a larger circle, or make smaller blooms by using a smaller circle. Depending on the fabric used, larger circles may require more petals to have a full bloom, and smaller circles may require fewer. Using different-size blooms in groups can add even more flair to your larger projects.

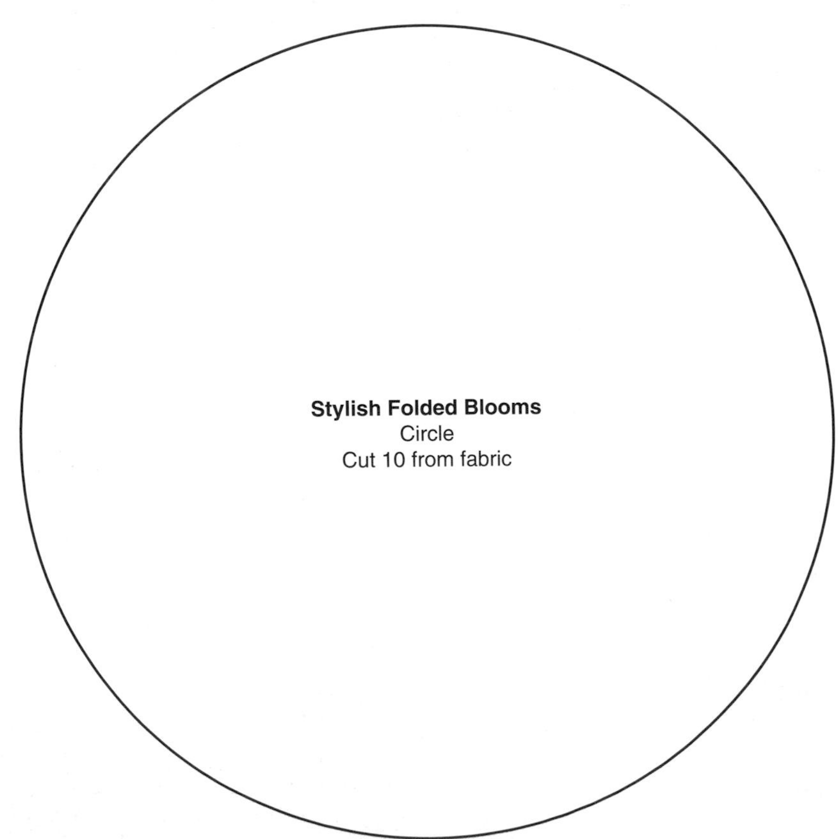
Stylish Folded Blooms
Circle
Cut 10 from fabric

Lovely Looped Blooms

Finished Size
Approximately 3 inches in diameter

Materials
- 4½ x 12-inch piece craft or wool felt
- Hot-glue gun and glue sticks
- Basic sewing supplies and equipment

Cutting
From felt:
Cut two 2¼ x 12-inch strips.

Assembly

1. Fold a 2¼ x 11¾-inch strip in half lengthwise, wrong sides together. Stitch or glue the long edges together.

2. Cut a ¼-inch piece off the end of the folded strip and set aside (Figure 1). Cut the folded edge of the rest of the strip into ¼-inch increments, stopping ¼ inch from stitching (or glue line) as shown in Figure 1.

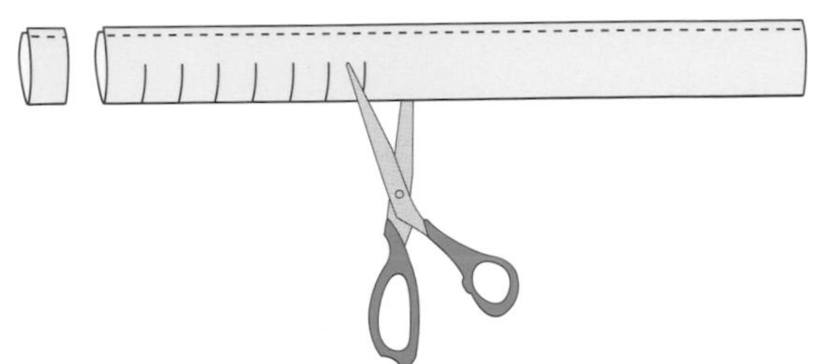

Figure 1

3. Beginning with the left end of the cut strip, roll and glue the base of the petals together as shown.

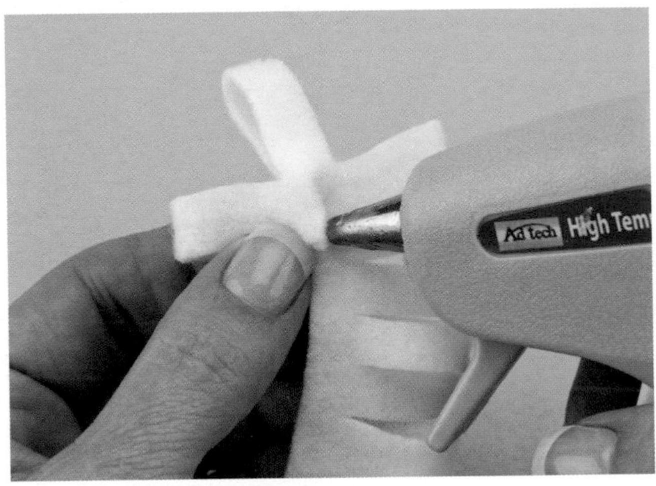

4. Make full rotations with the strip, rotating clockwise and gluing to the bottom of the flower as you rotate.

5. Continue to wrap strip then glue end to secure. Glue a set-aside ¼ x 2¼-inch piece loop to the center of the flower to complete the Lovely Looped Bloom. ■

Tip

Hot-glue Lovely Looped Blooms to the toes of shoes or flip-flops, or add to hair clips, bags and backpacks. You could also hand-stitch a pin back to the center back of the flower to use as a jacket or sweater pin.

Pretty Poinsettias

Finished Size
4–4½-inches in diameter

Materials
- 18 x 22-inch piece cotton, wool or felt
- Liquid fabric stiffener
- Foam paintbrush
- Hot-glue gun and glue sticks
- Gold seed beads or 6–8mm white pearl beads
- 6 inches ⅛-inch-wide ribbon (optional)
- Pin back (optional)
- Basic sewing supplies and equipment

Fabric Preparation
Treating some fabrics with a liquid fabric stiffener makes them easier to cut and bend. For cotton, brush the liquid stiffener onto both sides of fabric with foam brush, following the manufacturer's directions. Allow to dry completely. Wool and felt do not need to be treated.

Cutting

From cotton, wool or felt:
Make small, medium and large poinsettia templates using patterns provided. For one flower, trace one each small and medium poinsettia and two large poinsettias onto the right side of fabric (Figure 1). Cut out on traced lines.

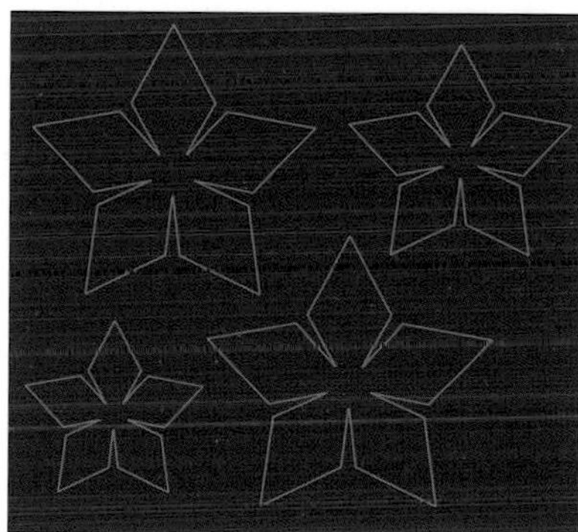

Figure 1

Assembly
1. Place a small dab of hot glue at the base of a petal (Figure 2).

Figure 2

2. Pinch the base of the petal and hold in place while glue cools (Figure 3).

Figure 3

3. Repeat steps 1 and 2 on all poinsettia petals.

4. Beginning with the large petals, stack and hot-glue layers together at center in descending order, staggering petal positions and finishing with small petals.

5. Add a small amount of hot glue to center of the small poinsettia and gently add gold or white beads for flower center.

6. Hot-glue a pin back to wrong side of poinsettia flower to use as a brooch. To use as a Christmas tree ornament, hot-glue a ribbon loop to the top of the wrong side of the poinsettia. To use as a napkin ring, glue to a circle of elastic.

7. Repeat steps 1–6 to make more flowers as desired. ■

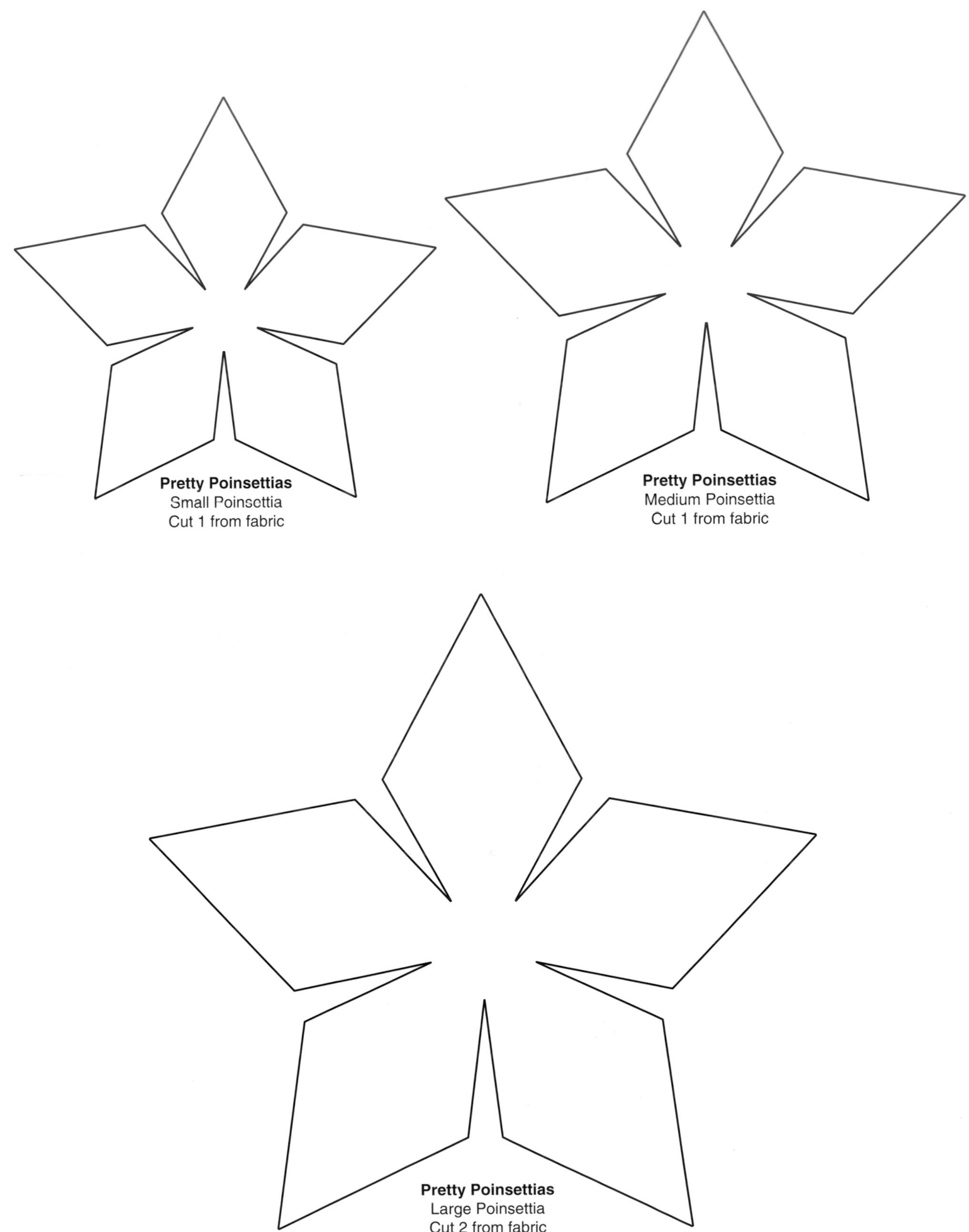
Pretty Poinsettias
Small Poinsettia
Cut 1 from fabric
Pretty Poinsettias
Medium Poinsettia
Cut 1 from fabric
Pretty Poinsettias
Large Poinsettia
Cut 2 from fabric

Pinched Blooms

Finished Size
Approximately 7 inches in diameter

Materials
- 18 x 22-inch piece craft or wool felt
- Hot-glue gun and glue sticks
- 3 (½-inch-diameter) ball buttons or beads
- Staple gun
- Basic sewing supplies and equipment

Cutting

From felt:
Using patterns provided, cut one each small, medium and large petals, and two extra-large petals.

Assembly
1. Place a small amount of hot-glue at the base of a single petal shape (Figure 1).

Figure 1

2. Quickly pinch the petal base together and hold until glue cools (Figure 2).

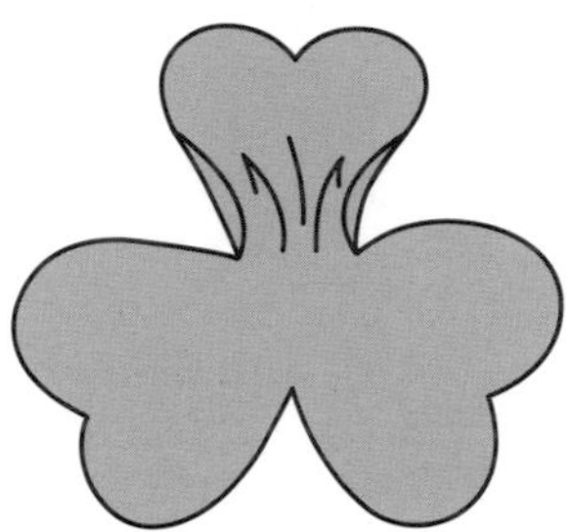

Figure 2

3. Repeat steps 1 and 2 on each petal on all sizes.

4. Beginning with the extra-large petals, stack and hot-glue layers together at center in descending order, staggering petal positions and finishing with small petals.

5. Hot-glue ball buttons or beads to flower center.

Tip
Hot-glue pinched blooms to the frame of a purchased magnetic message board, cork tiles or a precut framed or unframed cork board.

Amy Thomas
Dupont Parkview North
Grocery list
Bacon
Eggs
Milk
Cheese
pasta
Doctors
Apt.
11:30 FRI

Message Board

You Will Need

- ½ yard outdoor canvas print
- 12 x 12-inch stretcher frame
- 1 Pinched Bloom
- Hot-glue gun and glue sticks

Assembly

1. Construct stretcher frame according to manufacturer's instructions.

2. Lay the stretcher frame facedown on the back of the canvas print. Fold one edge of the canvas over the back of the frame and secure with staple.

3. Rotate the canvas 180 degrees. Pull the canvas tight and wrap around the opposite side of the frame. Staple in place.

4. Rotate the canvas 90 degrees and repeat the process, stretching and stapling on each side. Check the front to ensure your stretch is straight and there are no diagonal puckers.

5. Continue to stretch the canvas on opposite sides of the frame, working toward the corners.

Tip

Make your canvas message board a super-easy project with a purchased pre-stretched canvas!

Cut a piece of outdoor canvas print at least 6 inches larger all around than the purchased pre-stretched canvas.

Spray the wrong side of the outdoor canvas print with spray fabric adhesive.

Smooth canvas over pre-stretched canvas top and sides, folding corners and securing with hot-glue on back.

Attach one or more pinched blooms to board with hot-glue depending on size.

6. Fold the corners and staple on the back. Trim excess canvas as desired.

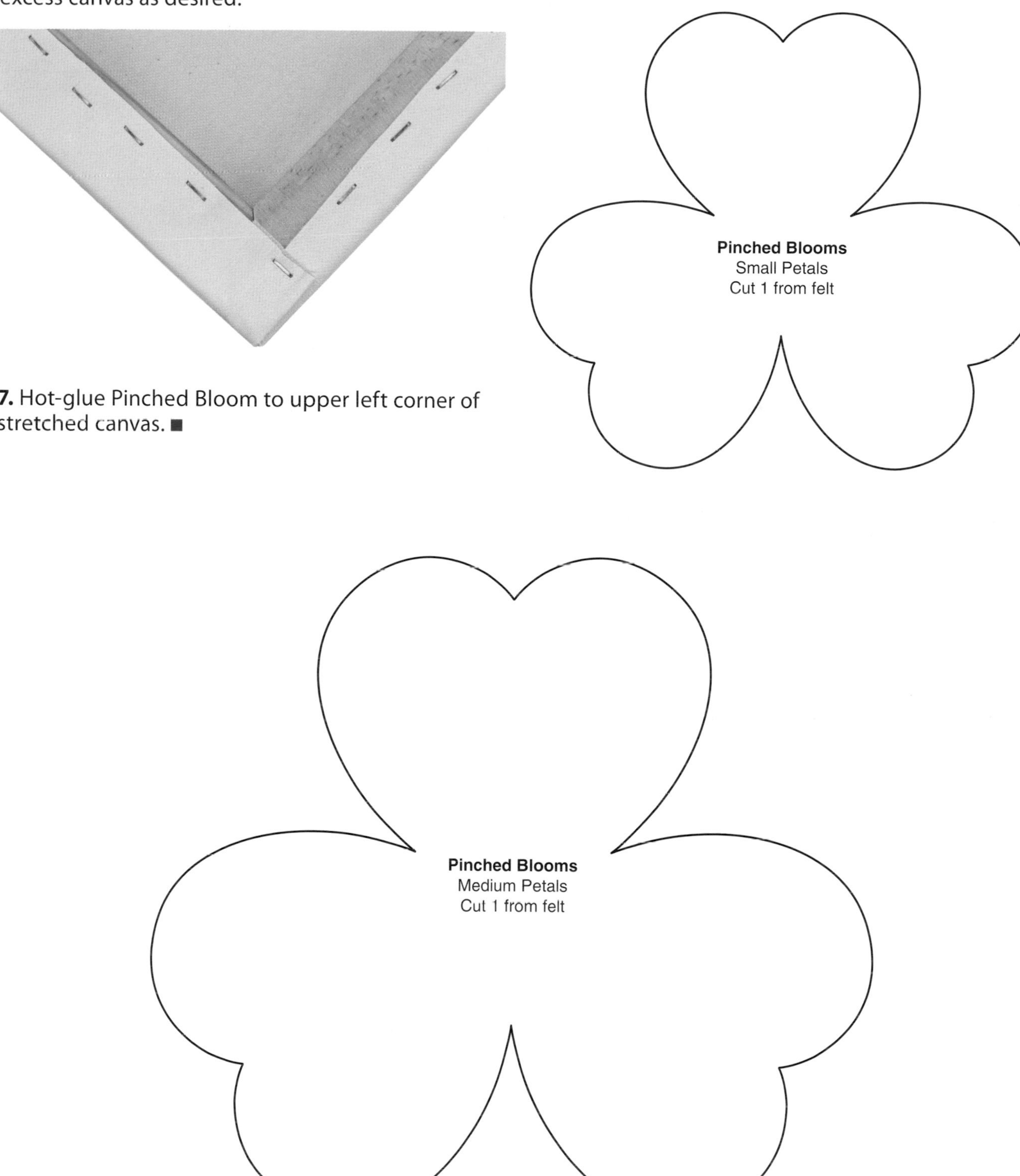

7. Hot-glue Pinched Bloom to upper left corner of stretched canvas. ■

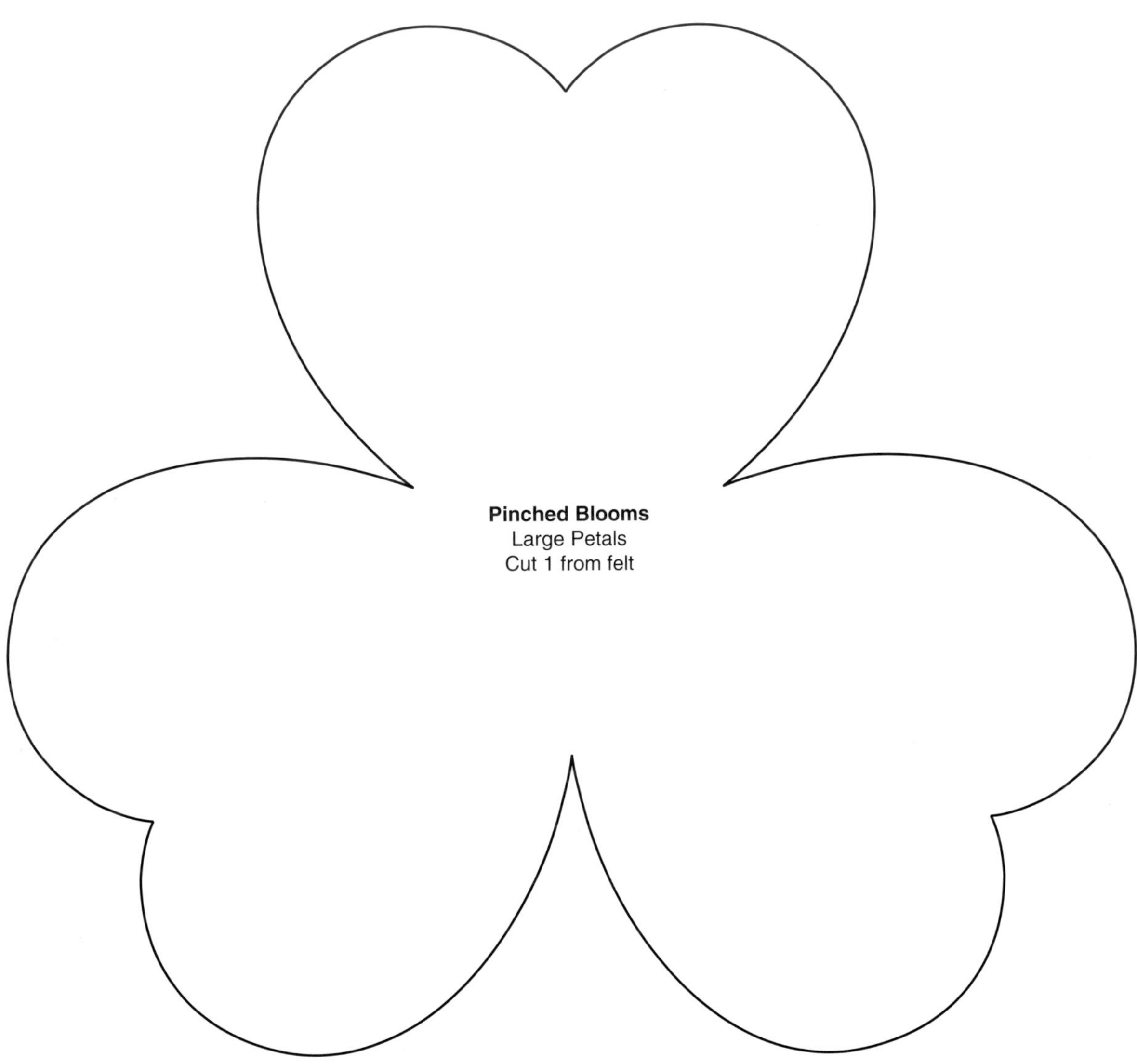
Pinched Blooms
Large Petals
Cut 1 from felt

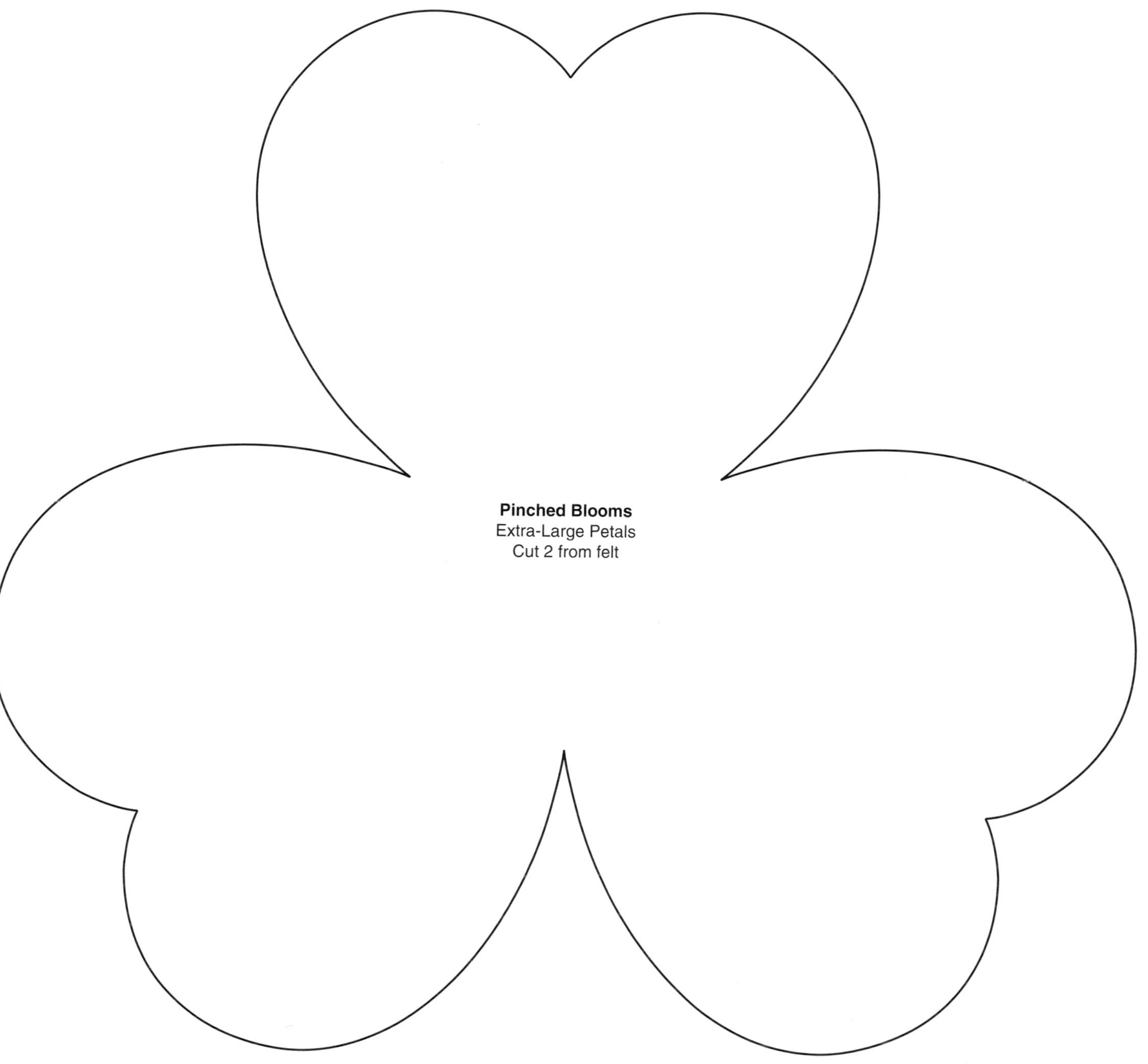
Pinched Blooms
Extra-Large Petals
Cut 2 from felt

Twist & Turn Flowers

Finished Size
Approximately 3 inches diameter

Materials
- ¼ yard fabric
- Felt scraps
- Hot-glue gun and glue sticks (optional)
- Decorative buttons or beads, up to 1-inch diameter
- Basic sewing supplies and equipment

Cutting
From fabric:
- Cut one 7½-inch-diameter circle using pattern provided.

From felt:
- Cut one 2¼-inch-diameter circle using pattern provided.

Tips

Use light- to medium-weight woven fabrics. It is best not to use sheers since they allow the back-side stitching to show through.

A quarter of a yard will yield five 3-inch-diameter flowers.

Assembly
1. To make a yo-yo, hand-sew a gathering stitch ⅛ inch from fabric circle edge with a knotted thread (Figure 1).

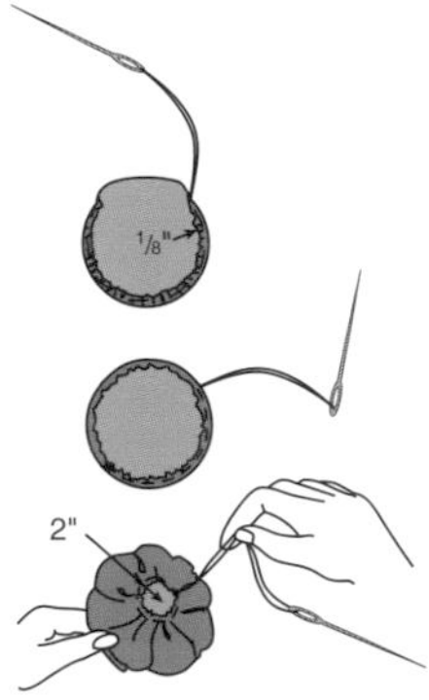

Figure 1

2. Pull thread to gather circle's edge to leave a 2-inch-diameter opening in yo-yo. Knot thread to secure and trim thread tail. Flatten yo-yo with gathered edge at center, again referring to Figure 1.

3. Hand-sew felt circle over center opening on yo-yo, catching only edges in stitching (Figure 2).

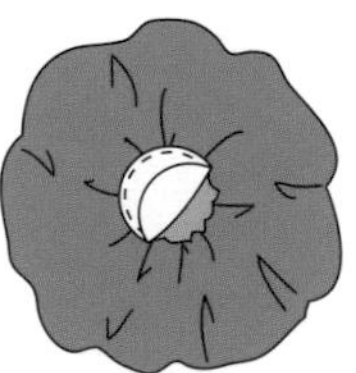

Figure 2

4. Grab center of yo-yo and felt circle with opposite hands and gently pull apart.

5. While still holding yo-yo and felt circle, twist the fabric counterclockwise as shown in Figure 3; push down toward felt circle to flatten.

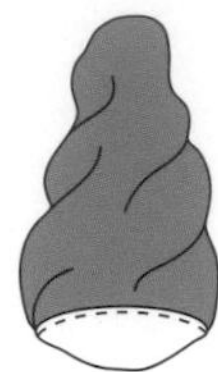

Figure 3

6. Hold twisted yo-yo in place and hand-sew three to four stitches through all thicknesses at center of yo-yo to hold in place (Figure 4). Knot thread and trim thread tail.

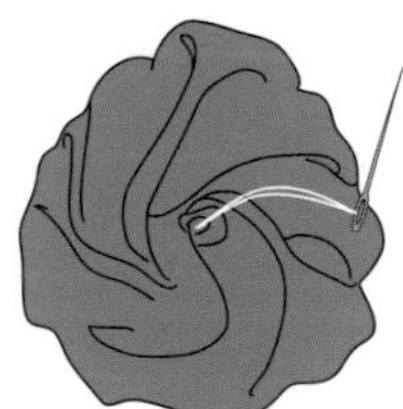

Figure 4

7. Hand-stitch or hot-glue decorative button or bead to flower center to complete.

Tip

Hand-stitching a button or bead in the center will help hold the twisted yo-yo in place.

Twist & Turn Belt

You Will Need

- Purchased or self-made wide belt
- 3 Twist & Turn Flowers
- Decorative button or bead embellishments (optional)

Assembly

1. Choose a fabric or elastic belt in your size that can be clasped in back or tied so that a buckle doesn't compete with your flower embellishments.

2. Try on belt to determine belt center front and mark with pin or fabric marker.

3. If using a stretch belt, hand-sew the Twist & Turn Flowers to the left or right of the belt center in a triangular pattern. If desired, attach extra decorative button or bead embellishments.

4. If using a fabric belt, hand-sew or hot-glue flowers and extra embellishments in place. ■

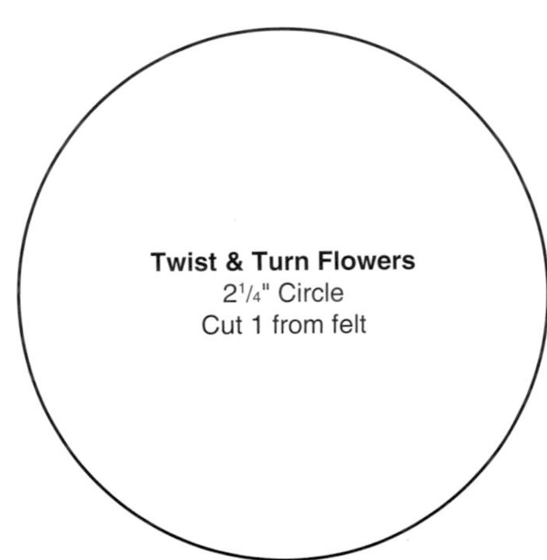

Twist & Turn Flowers
7$^{1}/_{2}$" Circle
Cut 1 from fabric

Friendship Blooms

Finished Size
Approximately 6 inches in diameter

Materials
- 3 (9 x 22-inch) pieces coordinating prints (A, B, C)
- 6 x 6-inch scraps burlap or netting
- 1-inch cover button
- Basic sewing supplies and equipment

Cutting

From prints A, B, C:
- Cut one 2 x 22-inch strip each.

From burlap or netting:
- Cut one 4½-inch-diameter circle using pattern provided.

Tip

Hot-glue or stitch a pin back to this large flower to make a great pin for sweaters, sweatshirts and hats. Or, decorate baskets, gift boxes or bags or hand bags. Give as gifts to your very best friends.

Assembly
1. Hand- or machine-stitch a gathering stitch ¼ inch from one long edge of each of the A, B and C strips (Figure 1). Backstitch at beginning of stitching and leave long tail at beginning and end of each strip.

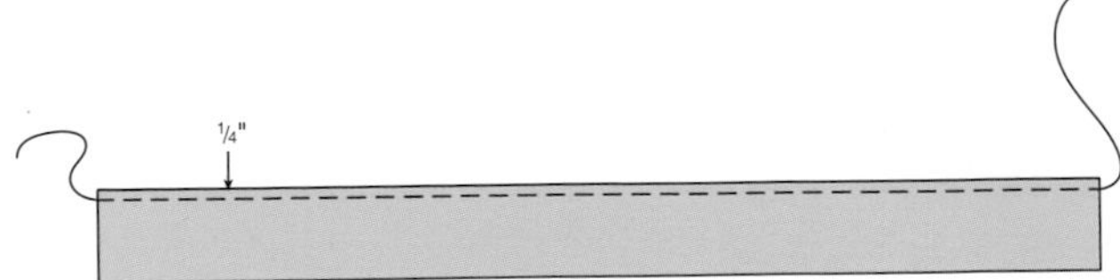

Figure 1

2. Gently pull end thread tails to gather strips into tight circles (Figure 2). On each strip, knot thread tails together to secure; trim thread tails.

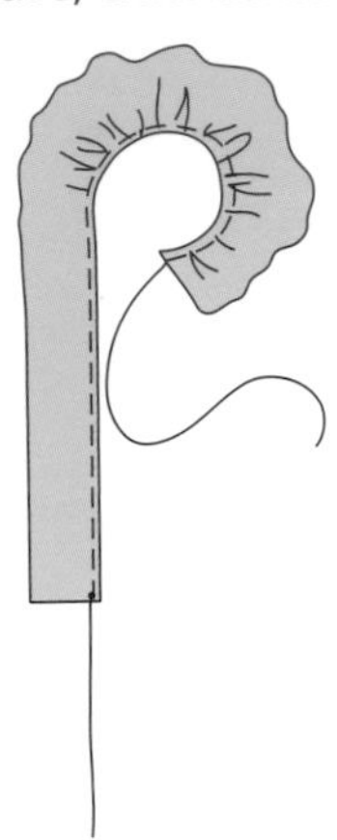

Figure 2

3. Layer gathered circles right sides up and centered, beginning with A, and then burlap or netting circle, B and C referring to photo.

4. Hand-stitch centers together through all layers.

5. Cover 1-inch button following manufacturer's instructions and using fabric B scraps.

6. Sew button to flower center through all layers. ■

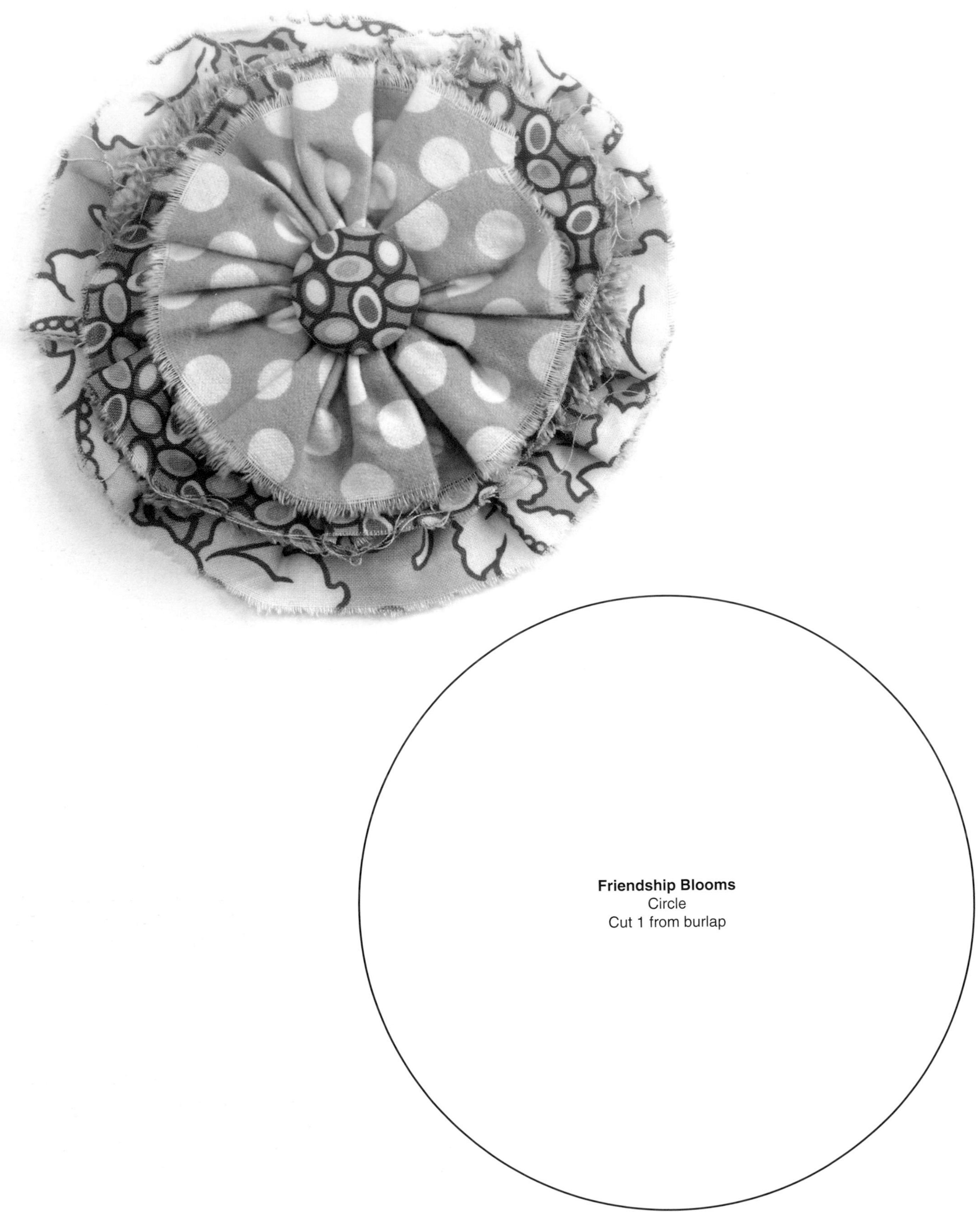
Friendship Blooms
Circle
Cut 1 from burlap

Canvas Petals

Finished Size

Approximately 8 inches in diameter

Materials

- 2 coordinating fat quarters
- ½ yard cream or white canvas
- ½ yard fusible fleece
- 1½-inch-diameter decorative button
- Template material
- Temporary fabric spray adhesive
- Black ink pad
- Stamp(s) of your choice
- Basic sewing supplies and equipment

Cutting

From fusible fleece:

- Cut two 18 x 22-inch rectangles.

From canvas:

- Cut two 18 x 22-inch rectangles.

Assembly

1. Fuse a fleece rectangle to the wrong side of each fat quarter following manufacturer's instructions.

2. Position canvas rectangles on covered flat surface. Spray canvas with temporary fabric spray adhesive.

3. Position and smooth fused fabric rectangles onto canvas rectangles fleece side down (Figure 1).

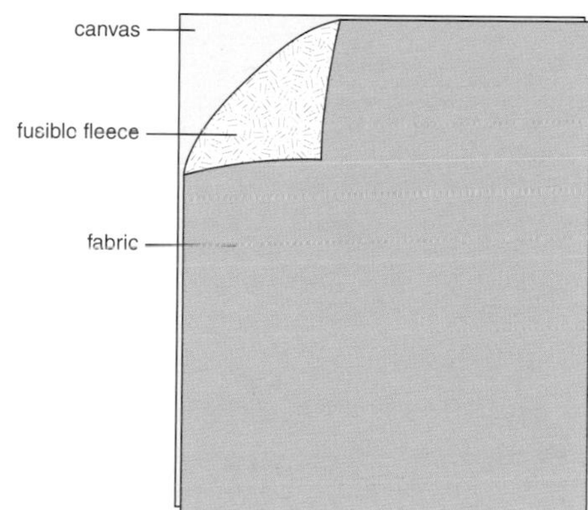

Figure 1

4. Prepare template for petal from pattern provided. Trace a total of nine petals onto both fabric/canvas rectangles with a fabric marker (Figure 2).

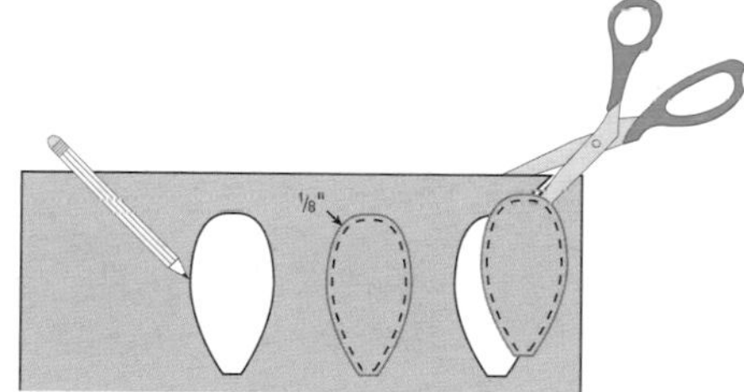

Figure 2

5. Stitch approximately ⅛ inch inside traced lines as shown in Figure 2. Cut out petals on traced line referring again to Figure 2.

Tip

Think about fabric colors and designs when choosing fabric for Canvas Petals. This flower is embellished with stamping, so choose lighter colors and more open designs.

6. Stitch parallel concentric petal shapes in the petal centers or as desired (Figure 3).

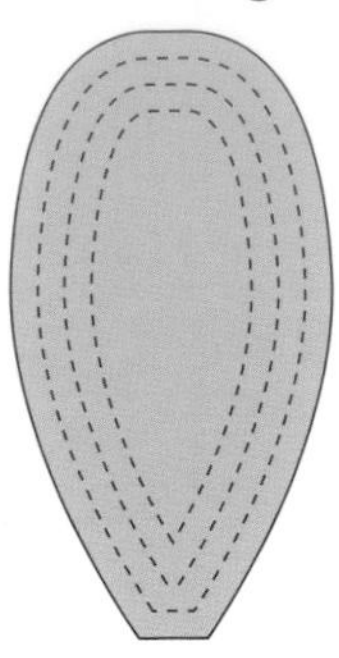

Figure 3

7. Stamp either the canvas or fabric sides of the petals for another layer of embellishment. Follow stamping instructions from the stamp manufacturer. Use the stamped sides as the right side of the petals.

8. Pinch the right side bottom end of a petal in half and hand-sew together at bottom edge with several stitches (Figure 4); knot thread and trim thread tails. Repeat for all petals.

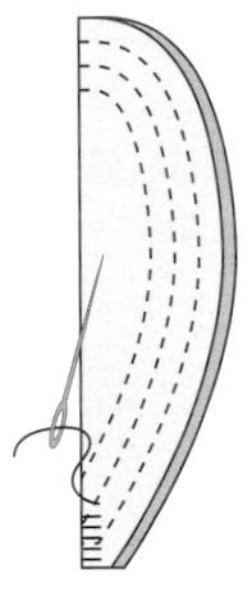

Figure 4

Figure 5

9. Hand-sew five petals together at bottom in a circle to make first petal layer of flower (Figure 5).

10. Hand-sew a second layer of petals on top. Stagger petal positions and stitch at petal bottoms stitching through all layers (Figure 6).

Figure 6

11. Stitch a large decorative button to center of flower.

Canvas Flower Pillow

You Will Need

- 16-inch or larger purchased or handmade pillow
- 1 Canvas Flower

Assembly

Hand-sew a Canvas Flower to one corner of pillow. Leave petals free at outside edges. ■

Tip

This flower is large! Use it to embellish items that are big enough not to be overpowered by its size. Large pillows and tote bags are good choices.

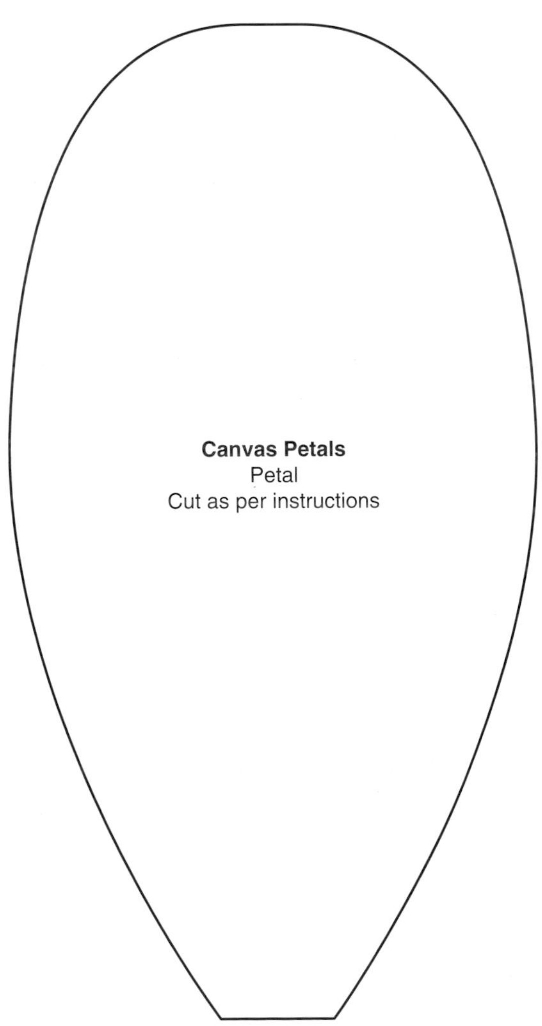

Rickrack Rings

Finished Size
Approximately 1¼ inches in diameter

Materials
- 2 (10-inch) lengths medium rickrack
- Matching thread
- Embossing powder and accessories
- Nonstick craft mat
- Tweezers
- Basic sewing supplies and equipment

Assembly
1. Layer one end of each rickrack length together and hand-sew several stitches through both layers to secure beginning of rickrack strip.

2. Carefully twist the two rickrack lengths together, intertwining the ridges.

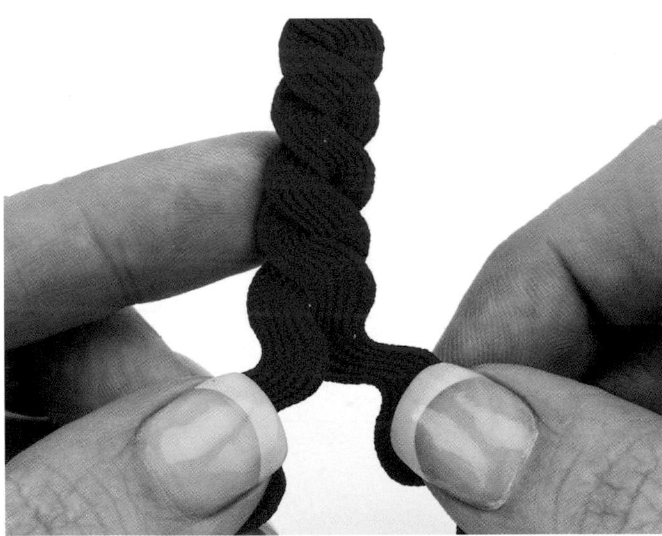

3. When lengths are twisted together, hand-sew several stitches through both layers to secure strip end. Do not trim thread.

4. Beginning at end with thread and needle still attached, roll one end of intertwined rickrack. Make several revolutions.

5. Stitch through all revolutions, side to side, to keep rickrack from unrolling with thread from end of rickrack strip securing stitches.

6. Continue to roll and stitch to end of rickrack strip. Stitch strip end to back of rolled rickrack. Knot and trim thread.

7. Gently bend back the top of each round of rickrack to form the flower.

8. Prepare the embossing powder following manufacturer's instructions. You will need to melt enough embossing powder to allow you to completely immerse the flower.

9. Grip back of flower with tweezers and dip flower in embossing liquid to cover fully.

10. Remove flower from liquid and allow excess liquid to drip off into melting pan.

11. Place flower on nonstick craft mat until completely cooled and hardened.

Rickrack Ring

You Will Need

- Ring blank your size
- 1 Rickrack Flower
- Hot-glue gun and glue sticks

Assembly

Hot-glue Rickrack Flower to ring blank base and allow to cool and harden. ■

Tips

These embossed flowers are just the right size to hot-glue a single flower to a hairpin blank or groups of flowers to barrettes.

Hot-glue them to flat covered buttons for whimsical buttons.

Add them to plain-Jane desk accessories like pencil boxes or business card holders.

Or use them to anchor a swag ribbon or fabric trim to a basket.

Rolled Roses

Finished Size
Made to size

Materials
- ⅛ yard woven fabric
- Felt scraps
- Hot-glue gun and glue sticks
- Basic sewing supplies and equipment

Cutting

From woven fabric:
- Tear or cut fabric into 1½-inch-wide strips. ***Note:*** *One-eighth yard will yield two to three strips. A 22-inch-long strip will make a 2½-inch-diameter flower.*

From felt:
- Cut a circle the size of the flower you wish to make.

Assembly
1. Tie a knot in one end of a fabric strip. Hot-glue the knot to the center of the felt circle.

2. Loosely twist the fabric strip while turning it around the knot.

Tips

Choose light- to medium-weight woven fabrics. Because the fabric strips used to make this flower are twisted, both sides of the fabric are visible.

With prints, this means there will be distinct differences in the brightness of the color variations. And with shiny fabrics, the surface changes from shiny to dull and adds depth to the flower.

3. Continue twisting and turning the fabric strip around the felt circle. Hot-glue in place as you turn the strip.

4. When you have covered the felt circle, if necessary, trim off any excess strip. Then tuck strip end between fabric and felt, and hot-glue to secure.

Rolled Roses Headband

You Will Need
- Purchased wide headband
- 3 Rolled Roses
- Hot-glue gun and glue sticks

Assembly
1. Make one each 3-, 2½- and 1½-inch diameter Rolled Roses in coordinating colors.

2. Hot-glue largest rose to side of headband. Attach medium-size rose on headband, slightly overlapping large rose.

3. Attach small rose to large rose and touching medium rose. ■

Tip

Smaller rolled roses made from lightweight woven fabric would make a nice embellishment to a sweater. Hand-sew flower in place instead of hot-gluing, either directly to the sweater neckline or to a washable felt circle and then attach it to sweater neckline.

Yo-Yo Bracelet

Finished Size

Your wrist measurement

Materials

- Variety 2–6-inch squares bright fabric scraps
- ⅓ yard 1½-inch-wide soft elastic
- ⅛–1-inch-wide buttons or jewels
- Thread
- Hot-glue gun and glue sticks
- Basic sewing supplies and equipment

Cutting

From elastic:

- Cut elastic to your wrist measurement plus 1½ inches for wearing ease. For example, for a 7-inch wrist measurement plus 1½ inches ease, you would cut an 8½-inch-long piece of elastic.

From bright fabric scraps:

Make templates using patterns provided. Trace and cut out 1½-, 2-, 3½- and 5-inch circles to make yo-yos. Begin by cutting at least three each 2-, 3½- and 5-inch circles and 12 (1½-inch) circles. ***Note:** You will need enough to cover the width and length of the elastic with yo-yos.*

Assembly

1. Stitch ends of elastic together using a ½-inch seam allowance (Figure 1).

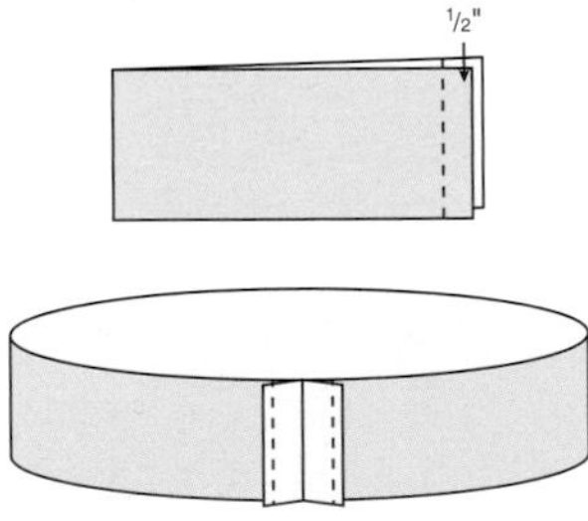

Figure 1

2. Pin seam open and stitch close to seam-allowance edges, referring again to Figure 1 to make elastic wristband. Set aside.

3. Refer to Figure 2 to prepare yo-yos. Hand-sew a gathering stitch ⅛ inch from circle edge, taking a backstitch at the beginning to secure the thread. Gently pull the thread to tightly gather the outer edge to the center of the circle. Flatten the circle and sew through all thicknesses to secure; knot and trim thread tails.

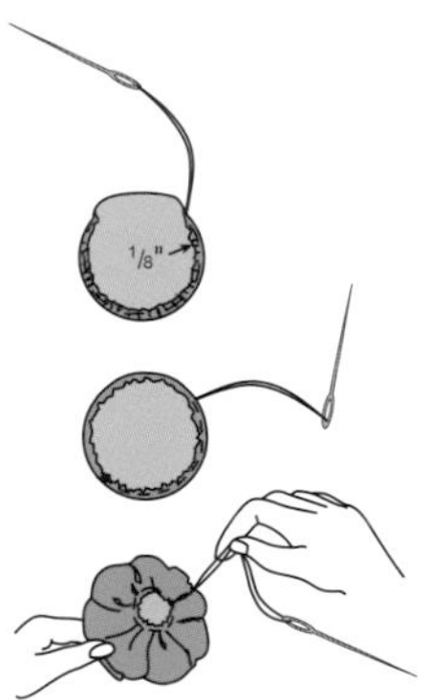

Figure 2

4. Glue or sew a button or jewel at yo-yo center that is large enough to cover raw edges.

5. Hot-glue a large yo-yo at center (directly opposite seam) of elastic wristband. Hold in place until glue cools and yo-yo flower adheres to band.

6. Continue adding yo-yo flowers to cover the wristband referring to Figure 3 and project photo. ***Note:** Glue larger flowers on first and fill in with the smaller flowers. Make more yo-yos if needed.* ■

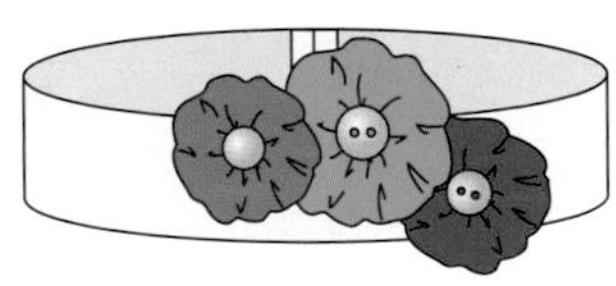

Figure 3

Yo-Yo Bracelet
$1^1/_2$" Circle
Cut as per instructions

Yo-Yo Bracelet
2" Circle
Cut as per instructions

Yo-Yo Bracelet
5" Circle
Cut as per instructions

Yo-Yo Bracelet
$3^1/_2$" Circle
Cut as per instructions

Pretty Petal Bowl

Finished Size
Approximately 11 inches in diameter by 4 inches deep

Materials
- 2 complementary fat quarters
- 1 package double-sided, heat-moldable fabric stabilizer
- Hot-glue gun and glue sticks
- Template material
- Rolling pin
- Basic sewing supplies and equipment

Assembly
1. Select one fat quarter for flower bowl and cut into two 11 x 18-inch rectangles. Press.

2. Layer the double-sided, moldable fusible fabric stabilizer between fabric rectangles, wrong sides together. Follow manufacturer's instructions to fuse layers together.

3. Prepare flower bowl base and petal templates from patterns provided.

Tip
Heat-moldable fabric stabilizers, like Inn-Spire™ Plus, allow you to shape fabric as well as giving it cardboard-like stability.

4. Use templates to trace six petals and one flower bowl base onto fused fabric (Figure 1). Cut out shapes on traced lines. Transfer center stitching line to each petal.

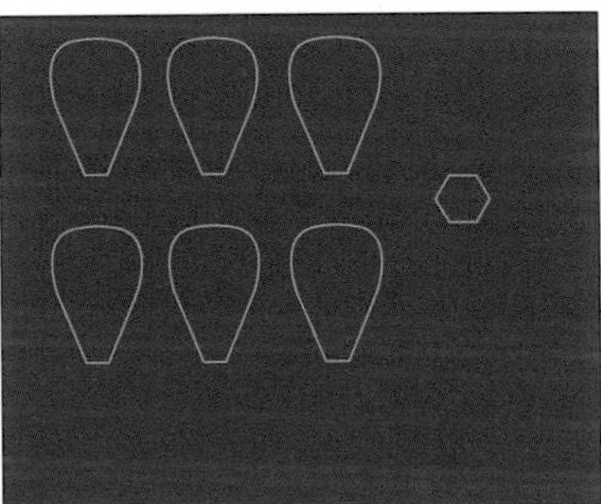

Figure 1

5. Set sewing machine to stitch a medium-density and -width zigzag stitch and insert a size 16 or 18 needle.

6. Using a complementary thread color, stitch on center stitching line on petals (Figure 2).

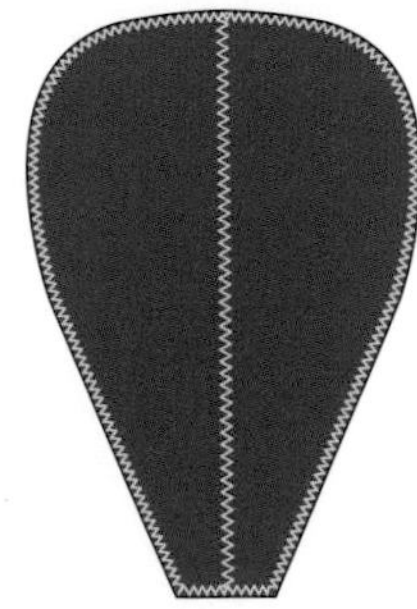

Figure 2

7. Stitch around outside edges of petals, again referring to Figure 2.

8. Heat a petal with iron and immediately curl rounded end of petal over rolling pin as shown in Figure 3. Hold in place until cool to give petal an outward curve. Repeat with all petals.

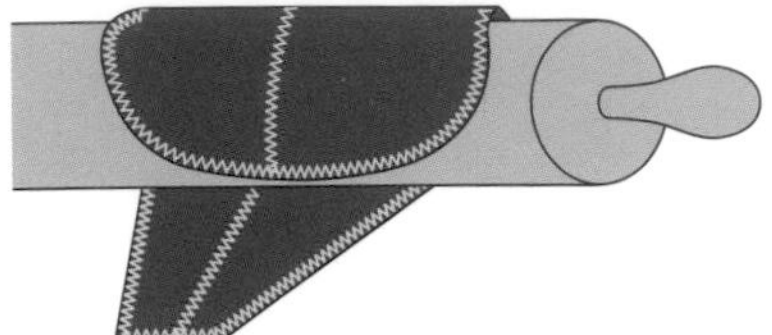

Figure 3

Tip

Heat softens the product for molding. So if you don't like the shape of your petal, then reheat, reshape and hold until cool!

9. Align straight bottom edge of petal with one side of flower bowl base. Zigzag stitch pieces together (Figure 4). ***Note:*** *If necessary, widen zigzag stitch to catch both pieces in stitching. Repeat to stitch all six petals to the base.*

Figure 4

10. Hot-glue petals together to form bowl by overlapping petals approximately ⅛ inch and about 1 inch up from base (Figure 5). Set aside.

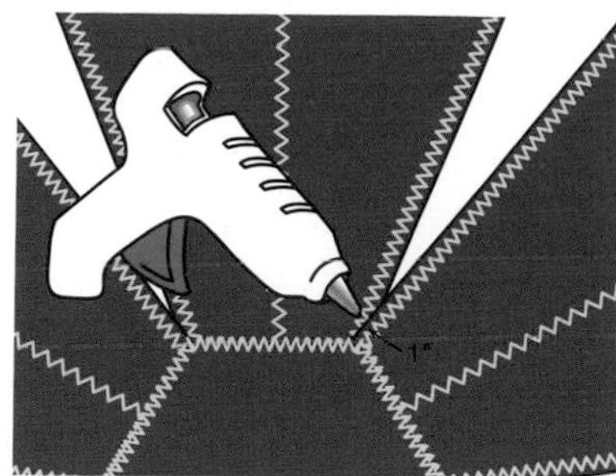

Figure 5

11. Repeat steps 1–7 using second fat quarter and leaf bowl base and leaf patterns.

12. Follow step 9 to stitch leaves to leaf bowl base.

13. To shape leaves, repeat step 8 except lay leaf lengthwise on rolling pin to curve outward lengthwise from base.

14. To complete trinket bowl, nest and hot-glue flower bowl inside leaf bowl, alternating position of petals and leaves. ■

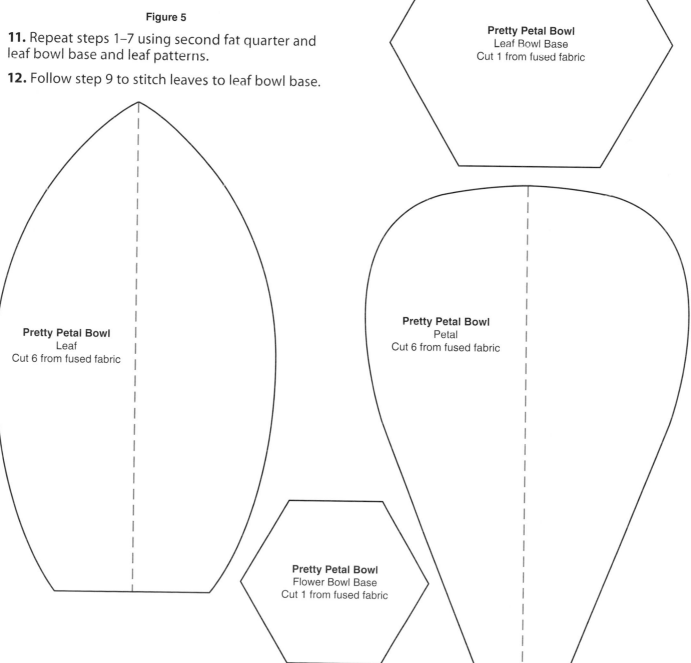

Pretty Petal Bowl
Leaf Bowl Base
Cut 1 from fused fabric

Pretty Petal Bowl
Leaf
Cut 6 from fused fabric

Pretty Petal Bowl
Petal
Cut 6 from fused fabric

Pretty Petal Bowl
Flower Bowl Base
Cut 1 from fused fabric

Spiral Roses

Finished Size
Approximately 1½ inches in diameter

Materials
- 1 fat quarter print
- Liquid fabric stiffener
- Foam paintbrush
- Cardboard
- Hot-glue gun and glue sticks
- Basic sewing supplies and equipment

Tip
Use 100 percent cotton fabric for these roses. Cotton absorbs the fabric stiffener well, and the wide variety of prints available will make beautiful multicolored roses that coordinate with anything!

Assembly
1. Press fat quarter to remove all wrinkles.

2. Follow liquid fabric stiffener manufacturer's instructions to coat both sides of the fat quarter. Hang to dry completely.

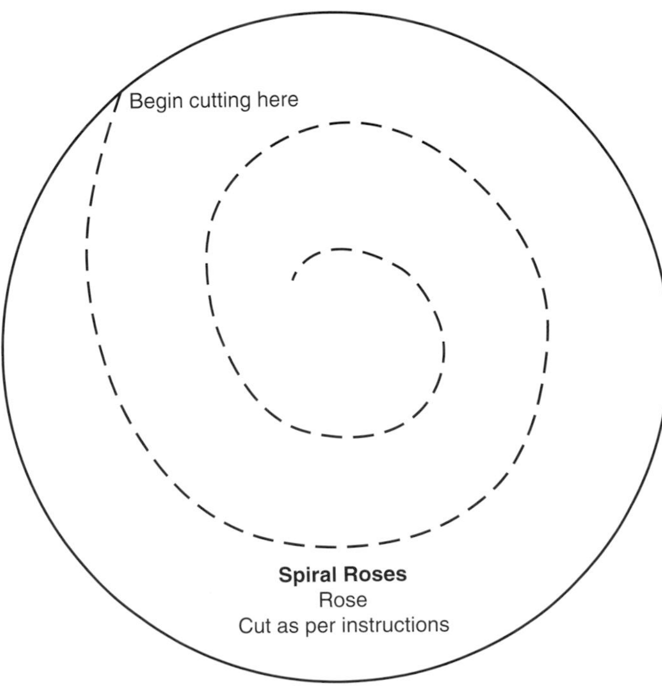

3. Prepare a cardboard circle template from pattern provided, transferring spiral dotted line to template.

4. Trace outer circle onto stiffened fabric and cut out on traced line. Transfer spiral dotted line to fabric circle.

5. Cut fabric circle in a spiral as marked (Figure 1), keeping cutting lines approximately ½ inch apart.

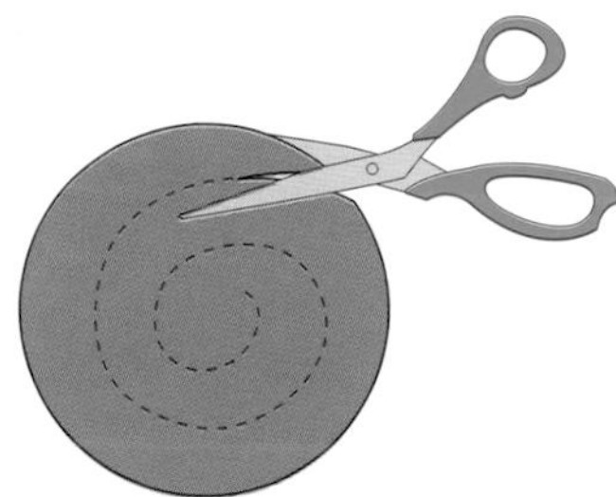

Figure 1

6. Beginning with outside end, roll spiral fabric strip to center of circle.

7. Place a small amount of hot glue at circle center while holding rolled strip. Allow rolled strip to relax into glue. Gently press in place.

Tip
Rolling and relaxing the spiral into the glue takes a little practice. Cut several spiral rose circle patterns from construction paper and make practice roses. Construction paper is about the same thickness as the stiffened fabric.

8. Repeat steps 4–7 to make more flowers.

Spiral Roses Picture Frame

You Will Need

- Small wide-edge picture frame
- 18–20 Spiral Roses
- Hot-glue gun and glue sticks

Assembly

Hot-glue Spiral Roses in rows across bottom and along left side of frame. ■

Tip

These roses work well on projects that will not have a lot of handling and will not need to be cleaned, just dusted. For example, add them to desk accessories, gift bags and boxes, and baskets.

Photo Index

6

4

9

10

13

17

20

26

30

33

36

38

40

43

46

Annie's™ *Bloom—A Collection of Fabric Flowers* is published by Annie's, 306 East Parr Road, Berne, IN 46711. Printed in USA.

ISBN: 978-1-59217-436-2

2 3 4 5 6 7 8 9